The Alienate
Rebuilding Your Life After Your
Copyright © 2015
All rights re

No part of this book may be reproduced or utilized in any form or by any means without written permission from the author.

Disclaimer

From the Author:

I am not a legal, medical, or mental health professional or expert. The content herein is based on personal observations and experiences which formed my opinions and beliefs, and those are what I share and discuss.

You are responsible for the health and safety of yourself and your charges. If you are in need of medical/mental health, legal, or any type of assistance, always consult professionally credentialed sources.

This book is intended for women who are no longer in danger from an abusive relationship.

Dedication

For Robin and her mom.

And ye shall seek me, and find me, when ye shall search for me with all your heart. - Jeremiah 29:13

You're trying to rebuild your life...

After escaping an abusive relationship, you might find that you have profound issues to contend with.

Your emotions can run the gamut from exhilaration to panic, from residual anger to guilt. You may be in mourning one minute, and filled with optimism the next. And if your social skills have deteriorated, it will be hard to connect with others. Another common aftereffect is a feeling of impending doom, which is the old conditioning of waiting for the hammer to fall, even though the abuser is gone and the danger has passed.

Yet another post-abuse issue is the confusion and inner conflict that was created by the years spent having to lie about your life, which is a habit that's hard to break. Simply put, it's difficult to relax and just be who you are.

Your health may be in question, as well. You probably should see a doctor and get a full physical, because even if you managed to maintain self-care, the stress you've endured can take a toll on you physically.

Hopefully, you have a support system around you - and now that you no longer have to filter your life through the batterer's perspective, you can start rebuilding.

But what if you now find that your children are rejecting you?

The Alienated Mother

*"Yesterday was my birthday. My **birthday**, and they didn't even call me. I waited by the phone all day."*

A client said that several years ago. At the time, she was almost two years beyond her acrimonious divorce, one which came after over two decades of enduring a violent male.

We spent most of that afternoon together, during which time she ran the emotional gamut - from outraged declarations of total indifference to her situation, to tearful recounting of good memories with her children. I felt horrible for her, and I had some difficulty controlling my own anger at her ex. And yes, at her children, as well.

Afterward, I began to take serious notice of this trend among young adults who grow up observing their fathers abuse their mothers, and then - upon reaching their late teen/young adult years - take a hard turn into rejecting them. Not their fathers: their *mothers*.

I'm not talking about the spate of rebellious foolishness that the experts insist is normal. (It's not, but that's another topic.) I'm talking about a child's full-throated condemnation of his/her primary emotional connection: a mindset and subsequent lifestyle of contempt for the woman who brought them to life. You don't hear about it often, because abusive fathers are trending toward the pretense that it happens only to *them*, and that evil mothers are the ones perpetuating it. They've even made a cause célèbre out of it (and a highly profitable industry has been created from it). They call it "Parental Alienation Syndrome."

I'm more interested in **Maternal** Alienation Syndrome (MAS), because it seems to be happening quite often with kids who grow up in abusive homes - that they wind up rejecting their mothers. It's so common an experience among the battered women I've talked with that I got frustrated enough to write a novel about it. Alienated mothers can, and often do, completely lose themselves inside their misery.

If you haven't suffered the anguish of spending your life enduring an abuser, and then losing your child's respect, love, and trust as a result, then the rest of this book won't make much sense to you. Still, it may give you some insight into the hell that so many mothers are trying to survive, in a culture that has turned largely contemptuous toward women while becoming devoted to the notion that fathers' rights trump all.

If you do know what I'm talking about: first, I'm so very sorry; and second, read on, because you need to keep living. And I'd like you to live well. Not just "as well as possible," but to live a life that has meaning to you.

You have a right to that. You've earned it. I'm not going to tell you how to win your children back into your life, because that may never happen; further, I'm not going to put on kid gloves to discuss this - because you've had the courage to survive an awful lot, and you retain enough hope to be reading this now.

The mother, the *person* you are is not defined by the opinions, beliefs, and responses of others, and you need to remember yourself. Even if your children do not.

It's time to take yourself back.

Sowing the Seeds of Maternal Alienation

If your ex-husband or partner was an abuser (which is the premise of this book), you run a chance of being alienated from your children after they become legal adults. Whether or not that's a permanent condition, no one knows; however, you have a right to reclaim your life, and to live it well.

Over the past few months, I've been following the journey of an alienated mother, one who posts daily on a social media site. She appears to be in total meltdown, like so many of these moms are. She rants incessantly - sometimes incoherently - about her ex, his new wife, and anyone and everyone whom she regards as their helpers. She defines alienation as something that begins after divorce. If hers is an authentic MAS situation, then I think she's wrong about that.

I had a few brief interactions with her, but she's beyond reach at this point. She's gone militant in her outrage and as a result, she's playing right into the hands of the (accused) alienators: her ex-husband and his new wife. If I could get her to listen, the following is what I'd say to her - and I'm thinking, maybe it would be useful to those of you who are aching to be able to freely love your children again.

In my opinion, the seeds of MAS are sown against a battered mother while she's living with the abusive husband. *Not after.* While you're preoccupied with trying to hold some semblance of a normal life together for your kids, they're learning from their father that you don't have any power, that you're kind of unbalanced, and that you don't really matter anyway. And they don't see you for what you really are: they believe that you're weak.

Some children will try to protect their mother until they burn out; others will turn away, repulsed. But with your focus going in one direction and theirs going in another, the time may come when you realize that at some point, you lost each other.

But at the same time they need you, and they love you, and the conflict within them can grow to the point where they mentally and emotionally throw their hands in the air and walk away. Although they've been brainwashed by their father's abuse, and the noncommittal silence of those around him, they do remember you somewhere in their hearts. And the confusion gets the best of them. Too often, their only method of breaking away - the only one they can live with - is to demonize you like their father does.

Besides, he's the path of least resistance. He can offer them the easy answers that they need as to why their family came apart, and why it was that you were so mistreated by him. Gradually, the mistreatment that they witnessed mutates in their minds, going from *abuse* to *consequence:* the natural result of what a rotten wife and mother you were, and therefore, you deserved what you got. And by the way, the first cousin of that kind of resolution is the belief that *you* wrecked their childhoods through your myriad of deficiencies.

More than that, the ex-husband often finds a replacement wife relatively quickly, and sets up what looks like a normal, happy life - the life that your children craved as they grew up in his home. That's a huge message to the kids, make no mistake about it. Since Dad appears to be able to have that contentment and normalcy with a different wife, it follows naturally that Mom was the problem.

Okay, enough about what they feel. You got them up and out. What about you?

You can shoot yourself in the foot by actually becoming the problem. You can't be blamed for that - not initially - because a lot of gaslighting happens in an alienation game, and an abuser can bait you into such despair and ugliness that you help to create your own downfall. Also, as most of your energies during the marriage went to the preservation and protection of your children, you probably lost track of not only your own needs, but the reality of what was happening to your kids.

And after you left the abuser, you know that you had a period of time where you had to reinvent a life for yourself, and probably not much real help in doing so.

Then the kids walked away, filled with contempt for you, and you can't get your legs under you again as you rail against what is a very real injustice. Take some time to do the crying and the venting, and to mourn the absence of reality within the perceptions of others.

Then get honest about a few things, because you need to make a choice: you can either crawl into your cave and stay there, or you can embrace the truths that will help you to build a better life than you thought possible - the very truths that you want others to see. You'll confront them when you stop being ashamed of how you feel, and address yourself head-on.

Dealing With Your Emotions

Here's what you may be feeling:

Pain

Of course.

You're excluded. That kind of anguish is bad enough; but life is going by, and you miss them. They don't share their lives with you, and you can't share yours with them. The memories of the life you lived with your kids feels like a hard lump in your stomach.

You're in a place of constant mourning, and it's becoming a permanent state of being, because you can't find your way through the stages of grieving - and that's probably the reason that you're stuck. Your children are out there someplace, and you can't let go of the hope that they'll come back. You're in limbo.

You've experienced some very real losses here, with the most poignant being the loss of your dreams, and that's what you need to confront and then mourn.

Every holiday, every birthday, every special occasion is drowned inside the pain of reliving the moment when you realized that your children didn't recognize you or remember you at all. I knew one woman who told me she felt "erased," because the very memories she once thought she would cherish were too painful for her to recall. Simply coming across an old picture of her children, or hearing a song that reminded her of them, could set off a crying jag that lasted all day.

If you feel that way, then think about this: those memories belong to you. If you decide that they're nothing but hurtful and mocking - instead of the precious threads of the tapestry of life that you made for your children - then you're erasing *yourself*.

Read that last line again.

You're actually taking over where the abuser leaves off, because he wants you to be erased. You could very well be helping him with that. As you mentally superimpose your children's hateful comments on top of your favorite pictures of them, you're setting the stage for agreeing with your ex that you were insignificant. Meaningless. That a mother's love can be suffocated under the heavy hand of his revenge.

And the last thing you want to do is to be your ex's ally, let alone agree with him about who and what you are, the value of how you lived your life, or let his efforts to alienate you strip you of your memories.

I'm in no way minimizing the pain of being shunned. I get it. It feels like the end of a world which you can't comprehend, an injustice and a betrayal that can never be remedied. But don't renounce your own history with your children just to avoid the truth of your life. If you do, you'll never come to realize just how heroic you were - and are.

Shame

You say to yourself, *My family is a mess. My children hate me. I'm a freak.*

Your family *is* a mess, and you may be exhausted from how long that's been the case. But do the kids really hate you? Or do they hate the fact that their family is a mess now, and always was? Are they as exhausted as you are?

Give them the space they need (easier said than done, I know, and we'll discuss how to do that later); but far more important, make sure that you're afforded the space that *you* need, because you were on the front lines of the chaos for a long time. You need to build yourself and your life again, and condemnation from anyone - including the kids, and including *you* - is not to be tolerated. You have an obligation to yourself to guard your heart, and that includes monitoring your inner dialogue.

Be aware of how you talk to yourself, because you've been torn down and blamed for too much already. Keep in the front of your mind the truth about who it really was who made the family such a mess, so when those shaming thoughts hit, you can be very deliberate in combating them. Refute them out loud when you can, and always try to pinpoint the triggers. (Keeping a small journal handy will help enormously with that.)

One of the major triggers of shame is envy. For example, if you're on the phone with a friend who's filling you in on her family and their happy holiday plans, you'll likely feel that jolt of pain in your stomach - the paralyzing envy that mixes with the anger of a vast injustice. Gracefully end the call, and then write down what you're feeling, the circumstances around it, and what you're saying to yourself. After several entries, you'll see the pattern of the experiences that deflate you, as well as your responses.

But don't avoid these experiences, because that will lead you into isolation. Instead, use those moments to form a protective shield for yourself. Not a wall: a *shield* - something you can place between yourself and the pain. For example, it may be that much of your pain at these times comes from the inability to give love to your children, or jealousy, or anger at the ex, and then you feel helpless. You start criticizing yourself, or perhaps you rage inside at how unfair it all is - and that's where you get stuck inside your emotions.

As you start to understand the pattern, you can then develop a plan that includes deliberate countermeasures that you use to address your needs. Even though you might feel empty, you'll find that giving of yourself is very healing. Try putting together a care package for the homeless, or donating to a food pantry. Volunteer for a cause you believe in. Adopt an elderly neighbor who's in need. In other words, share the love in your heart with others. Don't hold it in.

Keep in mind that at the point of an interaction where you feel envy, you'll also feel diminished, even inferior - and then, the easiest place to go to in your mind is straight to shame.

I use the word "easiest" because shame has an element of personal power to it. It comes from believing that you had or have some control over being alienated, which means you can affect the outcome. There is a sideways-kind of comfort in that belief. After all, if you're the one who drove your children away, then it logically follows that you can also do something to make things right again.

You can't. You don't have that power. It may be true that the most maddening aspect of MAS is in the fact that there's precious little you can do to win your children back, because there are forces working against you that you have no access to, and you have few opportunities to discredit them. As a result, your kids don't trust you because they don't fully remember you.

Know what? *You* may not remember you all that well, either. Not after the years of being defined by a male who terrorized you, and the lies you had to tell to others, to him, and to yourself in order to protect yourself and your children. Don't underestimate the damage caused by a life spent having to lie in order to survive, and how manipulating your environment can become a way of life. It's a hard habit to break; often, it takes some real effort to feel safe in being yourself again. But do the work, because lying just leads to more shame.

You need to recover your own identity, based in truth - and you need the time, space, and the clarity of perspective with which to do that.

Fear

You wonder what and how they're doing without you. You got used to protecting them. And if they're aligned with the batterer, you worry about the slurs that were directed at you in your absence today. You wonder if you'll ever get the chance to tell them all the things that they need to know. The feeling of powerlessness can be overwhelming.

The truth is, you have more power than you know.

This is a harsh reality, but one that you need to accept: they've made a choice, and you're out. Whether it's temporary or permanent, it's your current reality, and you need to deal with it.

So do your children, and they will.

Yes, they need you in their lives, and without you they're going to fall into their potholes without your input or the benefit of your wisdom; but another truth that you need to accept is the very fact that they're going to make mistakes, and they'll have to take their lumps. Just like we all do. More than that, a lot of their mistakes would have happened regardless of your station in their lives.

You are now, and will always be, their mother - and a good mother will allow her grown children to mess up, and then be there for the aftermath. You have to start healing yourself; not only for your sake, but because it may be that in the wake of some of their mistakes, they will seek you out.

Here's a question that you need to consider carefully: when they come looking for you, if they do, what do you want them to find?

They will encounter either a whimpering, lonely, desperate woman who wants only to keep them around, and that's *not* the mother they need; or they will find that the woman who raised them while braving the worst that life has to offer still stands strong and secure, has built a meaningful life for herself - and more than anything else, still loves her children enough to set the example of unwavering dignity in the face of oppression.

Your power - or lack of it - lies in the road that you choose to take.

Loneliness
You might feel like you've been fired, thinking along the lines of, *What do I do now, since my entire identity was - by necessity - their mother?*
Where do you belong?
Your life with the batterer was all about the kids, and your sacrifices preserved them; however, it also hindered you from forming honest and appropriate relationships with others.
Remember this: your existence in an abuser's home revolved around those kids because it had to. You were protecting, teaching, grasping for the peaceful, happy moments, and trying to create at least some good memories for them - all with an eye to a future where you would finally be free. At the moment, you may think that the rug has been pulled out from under you. And if that's how you're thinking, then your loneliness is going to become the place where you hide from reclaiming control of your life.
You're better than that. Stronger. The abuser is hoping that you never recover your sense of purpose - and wasn't isolating you one of his control games in the past? - but he no longer has that power unless you grant it to him.
Take an honest look at yourself. You survived a monstrous situation *and* the monster who created it, so don't hide your strength and wisdom from the world, because you earned those qualities the hard way. You had the brains and the tenacity to endure and survive the worst possible betrayal - an abusive mate - and you think you have nothing to offer now because your kids are rejecting you?
Take baby steps out into a world that needs you badly, and be good to yourself while you find your way to the places that need

you. Take it slowly. Rediscover your passions, the ones you nurtured and dreamed about before you got pulled into the batterer's craziness. What do you like? Dislike? Are there social issues or political causes that you care about? Are you able to honestly assess your own attitudes and opinions, or are you still in the prevent-abuse mode that you had to adopt while living with the abuser - the habit of filtering your thoughts and feelings through what the ex will do if he finds out?

That's a huge issue, one that's largely overlooked. Many times, a woman's post-abuse life is a confusing tangle of emotional extremes: worries feel like emergencies, fears become phobias, decisions present as insurmountable dilemmas. Trying to reclaim yourself in the midst of such mental chaos is difficult, so if you're floundering in your efforts to put your life back together, consider finding a professional therapist to talk to. (But make sure that the counselor you choose has a thorough understanding of the real dynamics of abuse, and a sympathetic ear for your particular issues.)

Try making actual lists and charts which reflect what you think and who you are, what you want to do, and who you want to be. Resurrect your old dreams, and start planning out how you can make them happen. Organize your plans, get to know yourself again - and lose the word "can't" from your vocabulary.

Then, get busy.

You'll still have the moments of longing and of missing your children. Sometimes those moments will knock the wind out of you, but the knowledge that you're needed elsewhere will tend to prop you up. Nothing dissolves loneliness like a sense of purpose.

Holidays and birthdays will be especially difficult, especially as you recall the traditions that you created for your children. Consider this carefully: those traditions belong to *you*, too. If you reject them, you'll be erasing another piece of yourself.

But it may be just too painful for you to hang their childhood ornaments on the Christmas tree, or bake the traditional birthday cake for yourself - at least, initially. Until you're steady enough to revisit those memories, use them as a template for sharing your traditions with others. A few ideas:

Give new holiday ornaments to a needy family, and keep one of them, every year, for your own tree. Or donate your own birthday - including your special cake - to an afternoon at a retirement home. If you're alone on Thanksgiving, volunteer at the local soup kitchen, and share your family's favorite recipes.

There's often a lethargy that develops with the alienation, and you might not feel like dragging yourself out of the house, especially on special days. Do it anyway. And decide that your efforts are not just temporary measures to get you through your pain: let them become extensions of your traditions, because you have every right to sustain them. After all, you created them.

Anger

Anger comes from the perceived violation of a relational contract between you and someone else, and it can take over every part of you.

The Anger of Betrayal

Do you feel betrayed by your children?

The thing is, your kids never signed on to a contract that promised to love, honor, and cherish you. Your ex vowed to do that, not your children. So why do you feel so betrayed by them?

It may be that the contract you feel they violated was their obligation to *respect* you.

Well, they don't respect you right now. And it's wrong, and it's what the abuser wants. It's what he taught them during the years that you were with him. But what are you going to do about it? Certainly, you don't want to respond with the same kind of petulant browbeating against him that he used against you, right?

You can say, "But he's the last person in my life who deserves any kind of respect," and that's a good point; however, it makes absolutely no difference to the choices you need to make now - or to the choices made by others, including your kids, about whether or not to respect you.

I don't mean to sound flippant. I know that the sudden turn these kids take is a devastating thing. In my experience with alienated mothers, the most common reactions from the children are that the daughters display a level of disgust for their mothers, while the sons tend to turn condescending. You can wind up feeling like everything you do, every word you speak is interpreted as more evidence of your incompetence - or worse, your evil nature.

What I'm saying is that you have two choices: you can either maintain your dignity, and continue to conduct yourself like a loving mother - which, of course, means that you put your kids' needs first, whatever those needs may be; or you can decide to compete with their father and with those who support him, and do whatever you can to win the approval of your children. Not only is that wrong for them, but turning into a sycophant is the fast track to giving away even more of yourself.

Besides, they need the same things that you do: they need you to be centered, compassionate, and strong.

What about those people who were on the periphery of the life you lived with the abuser? Are there family and friends who have abandoned you? If you feel betrayed by them, then you need to figure out the specifics of the contract that they violated in siding with him. Generally speaking, I believe that those who befriend, support, or remain neutral towards a batterer provide him with the power he needs to remain abusive. They have no moral right to do so, because they aren't the ones who endure the results.

The circumstances under which some people openly choose the batterer's side - and yes, this *is* about choosing sides - will vary; but the commonality among them usually comes down to a deliberate ignorance, which is at the core of cowardice. Which means the contract that they violated is one of the simple human decency that we all owe to each other.

Personally, I wouldn't allow such people in my life, no matter who they are. You may want to think about that as well.

Stop tying your self-worth to the opinions of others. The key to resolving the anger of betrayal is found in the fact that, clichéd as it may sound, you need to fully appreciate yourself. To do so, you have to conduct your life with the dignity that comes from living in truth - which includes being honest about yourself. You need to display the good (and forgive the not-so-good) within you.

Struggling through MAS, you're likely becoming well practiced in self-criticism, and sure - there are always some things you can do better. But are you realistic about your accomplishments? Do you acknowledge and appreciate your best attributes? Think about what you've endured, and the admiration you would feel for any other woman who survived what you have. You deserve the same respect.

The Anger of Being Cheated

Maybe you regard your life as an exercise in futility. All those years of devoting yourself to your children, and where are they now?

Don't misunderstand: you *have* been cheated. I'm not telling you that what you feel is invalid. I'm suggesting that you regard yourself differently, because inherent to the feeling of being cheated is a concurrent sense of having been a fool. And a consequence of regarding yourself as a fool is a defensive, even reflexive feeling of self-pity, and that can be crippling. It will blind you to the truth about yourself, which is the primary weapon of the alienator because it allows him to define you.

Here's a question: if you had it to do all over again, knowing you'd wind up where you are today, would you have abandoned those kids to your abusive ex?

Of course not. And that should tell you something more about who you really are - because the mother who would do it all again, even after being alienated, is a hero.

You brought them to life. You kept them safe. You taught them, and loved them, and gave them the best you could. Take comfort in that while you keep giving your best - to yourself and to others - and go forward with the attitude that the rest of your life is a story that has yet to be written.

The Anger of Being Slandered

There are a thousand tentacles sprouting out from this one, because one of the most devastating aspects of MAS is the onset of the false accusations.

Much of what you confront in dealing with MAS will be bald-faced lies about you. Many of those lies will be passively delivered by the ex, with your kids playing proxy. But be honest with yourself: not all of the accusations will be false.

Back when you were living with him, you did and said things that demeaned you, in your states of fear, panic, and outrage. Those moments can mushroom into the basis of a lot of condemnation in your kids' minds - and in yours, which is the central issue here - and they can become greatly exaggerated. Some can turn into false memories that lead to false accusations. Then, you start defending yourself against things you didn't do, while you try to redirect the focus onto how evil the abuser is and was.

Slander is like a spider web. You get the visual there. So when your child delivers a nasty, disrespectful comment or a false accusation, **be still.** *Think,* don't emote - you can do that later, in private - because if you react with anything beyond a noncommittal stare, a stock reply, and a fast topic change, you'll say something you regret. Something that diminishes you. Neither you nor your child should experience any more of that.

But if the issue or event that your child is discussing is factual, then you need to acknowledge it, apologize for it, and ask for forgiveness. In doing so, you'll not only lighten your conscience and build your self-esteem, but you'll be doing the exact opposite of what the ex and his supporters have likely been saying about you. That's a powerful response, one that makes a dent in the slander, and it will come into play as the future unfolds.

For the false accusations, the key is to be prepared, which is exactly what you will be if you *expect* to be lied to and lied about. Well before the situation is there in front of you, condition your responses. Practice them. Play devil's advocate with yourself - and while you're at it, ask yourself just how much you want to help your ex run you into the ground, and how much farther away you want to push your kids. Not to mention, how much more you want to degrade yourself.

The Anger of Injustice

Without a sense of the existence of justice, the soul withers. The very essence of faith turns on the concept of cause and effect, and it's hard-wired into our souls. Without it, life becomes a free-for-all of mistrust and despair, because nothing makes sense.

I'm a Christian. I can't imagine surviving MAS without Jesus Christ, and it's always difficult to work on this issue with women who don't have a core faith in Him.

That said, what you perceive as an absence of justice is really not your concern. Besides, you can't possibly mete out a justice that will truly satisfy you. Not after what he's cost you - not in the end. It simply isn't within your power to administer adequate discipline or punishment. Nor should you want to, because adopting his attitudes - which is what you'd be doing - won't make you feel better anyway. It's a waste of your valuable time and energy, and you have far better things to do.

More than that, your ex would enjoy watching you try to get even, because your attempts at revenge would mean that he still controls you. Being retaliatory enables and even enhances his well-practiced martyrdom, thereby giving him even more power over your children.

But enough about him. The point is, seeking revenge against evil serves only to suck you in to evil. Don't go there. It causes you to withdraw inside yourself, closing you off from a world that needs you.

When a moment of outrage hits you, use it as the impetus to give something of yourself to someone else, and then enjoy the feeling of having impacted the power of evil. You can find opportunities everywhere, if you stay open to the world around you, and it doesn't have to be a big event: I had one client who, when she felt herself falling into resentment, would go for a drive and look for chances to let people turn onto the road ahead of her. Another client would fill the bird feeders around her apartment complex. They said these small acts of kindness worked every time - it was like their burdens lifted completely away from them. It was freeing.

And if you truly embrace that kind of freedom, you'll open your mind to the possibilities for your own life.

Anger at God

I was shocked by the first Christian woman who came to me with the truth of her abusive husband. Not because she and her husband were believers - I mean, is there a better cover for an abuser than a church? - but because she was the best *actress* I ever saw. She was on-board, no issues, singing and praying and raising her hands every Sunday to receive God's blessings; yet she was so angry with God, I thought she might stroke out as she finally talked about it.

And all I could think was, *What? You think He doesn't know?*

If you're struggling with outrage towards the Father, you can white-knuckle your way through a pseudo-relationship with Him - or you can get real with Him. Talk about it. Ask Him to lead you, and to shout instructions directly into your ear if necessary. You don't have to be anyone but yourself with Him, and He will take it from there.

He knows all about this kind of pain, because He feels it every day. He, too, has been slandered and then alienated from His children, and far too many of His daughters have gone deaf to Him in their pain and mistrust - but He's still your Father.

Just like you're still your kids' mother. Right?

Mothering... Continued

Alienation is the ultimate test of your abilities as a mother, but you still have a job to do with those kids of yours, and it's the same job you always had: you need to set an example for them. You are responsible for showing them what dignity is - how a woman shows her strength in the face of the worst kind of adversity. That strength is made known in how deeply you still love them, and how you show it.

Some alienated mothers adopt a stance of feigned indifference, but you can't teach your children what love really is by ceasing to care. Some alienated mothers - like the woman I mentioned at the beginning of this book, the one on social media - get aggressive to the point of stalking, abusive behaviors. Acting like your ex...? Well, you get the dark irony there.

As a mother, you know that you will always have the responsibility of parenting your children. You do that, even in an MAS situation, by holding firm - for their best interests and for yours. Here's how:

Before anything else, **stop reacting**. **Do not** respond to anything negative or hurtful until your feelings have matured into thoughts, or you'll play right into the MAS games. Have stock responses on standby, phrases such as, "I'll certainly give that some thought," or "I see what you mean."

Second, develop an aversion - like a threat of anaphylaxis - to the **Three Com's:**

Competition (in other words, live and let live, and especially when it comes to the ex);

Complaining (build a life that you don't ever feel the need to whine about); and

Compromise (hang on to your principles like a series of lifelines - because they are).

Then, start taking those baby steps out into the world, ASAP.

Begin a journal for your children. Not about your pain and angst and fears, but about life. About the things you want them to know, mother-to-child. No matter the outcome of your situation, they'll need it one day. And when you are with them, be gentle but firm. Your children, too, are confused, hurt, and more needy than they'll ever acknowledge - and your inclination may be to parent them out of guilt or pity. Or both. Neither response is in their best interests, or yours.

Hold to your standards, but don't be militant with limits and boundaries. Expect melodramatic language from them, as well as baiting (which often takes the form of false accusations), and respond with concern and understanding - not shock, and definitely not defensiveness. Remember, if they have a legitimate complaint against you, you need to be open to hearing it. Take it seriously, offer an apology, and let them know that you'll be thinking about it. Ask for their input on how to make them feel better. With each encounter, you want them to be reassured of three things as they walk away: you love them unconditionally, you will always be there if they need you, and you all will be okay.

What they most need to understand, though - which they will do by watching you - is that while you would happily die for them, you can no longer *live* for them.

As your lives unfold, the value of that lesson will serve all of you well.

Finally, and only if you really need to (and eventually, you shouldn't), find a safe person to whom you can vent. *The keyword there is "safe."* If the ventee has anything at all (read that as **anything at all**) to do with the ex and/or your kids, even tangentially, then talking to that person about your issues is a great big "no."

I'm not saying that any of this will bring your children back to you. No one knows if that will ever happen. It may not. Sometimes, you'll still have those quiet moments at the end of the day, the times when you hear the echoes of your children's voices. You'll pull an old photo of them from a box, and you'll hear the laughter of their childhoods - and the sadness of your life without them will wash over you, sucking the air out of your lungs.

It will hurt. A lot.

When it starts to hurt, look up and thank God that He gave them to *you* to protect, because He knew that you were the only one who could. Then ask Him to take it over for you, because you know there's so much more to do, and you need to get busy.

Then pat yourself on the back, Mom. You're doing your best for them. You always have, and you always will.

Because you will forever be their mother, and that's what mothers do.

Now... Get Busy

A few final thoughts:

You probably noticed the theme running through this book: making sure you don't withdraw inside the pain of being alienated - because you have a life that matters to you, to the world, and to your children. The key is in keeping your mind and your heart open to what your life can be, by managing your emotions with an eye towards channeling them into good works.

What's happened to you is wrong. It's unjust, and it's rooted in evil; however, every time you refuse to relinquish your dignity, you heal a little more of yourself while you chip away at the alienator's games. Every time you reach out and do something that benefits others - in spite of having to live with the consequences of someone else's decision to hurt you - you strike another blow at the power of evil, and you reclaim another part of yourself.

And by the way, that's a great example for your children to follow, isn't it?

Use the following few pages to record some of the challenges you confront, how they're affecting you, and then - most important - what you will do to overcome them. It's a way to start creating your life plan.

Then keep this book as a reference for the future, because someday, you will want to look back at the road you traveled. You might want to revisit how you became such a wise, strong woman - and you never know who else might need to hear your story.

Mom's Journal

(Remember to include your victories, too.)

Mom's Journal

Mom's Journal

Mom's Journal

About the Author

"In general, I write about women's issues. But my passion in life is to change the way the culture regards battered women, and help them to reclaim their lives after escaping an abuser." - Jenna Brooks

A staunch Mothers Rights advocate, Jenna Brooks is a bestselling novelist, a seminar author and instructor, a columnist, and a professionally trained and certified coach, specializing in divorce, post-divorce, and Domestic Violence. She has a particular interest in the issues confronting Christian women, and is certified by The American Association of Christian Counselors.

The award-winning author of the *October Snow* series, Jenna is also the creator of several seminars and coaching processes. She is trained in Batterer Intervention, Trauma and Trauma Informed Care, and is a former state-certified Crisis Advocate and Domestic Violence Hotline veteran.

Jenna says, "I concentrate on advocacy for battered mothers because in my experience, the Family Court often takes up where an abuser leaves off. Too often, these women are every bit as injured by a paternalistic, even oppressive Family Court system as they are by an abuser. Their experiences in the court are simply another betrayal. As a society, we pay little attention to the outcome of battered mothers - both legally and culturally."

Jenna is a former columnist for *The Derry News* and *The Bangor Daily News*, and is the former host of "The Café" on WSMN Radio out of Nashua, NH. Her debut novel, OCTOBER SNOW, is the winner of the 2014 Readers Favorite Awards/Drama. Find her online at jennabrooks.weebly.com.

Also by Jenna Brooks

October Snow
The award-winning novel about the aftermath of abuse

An Early Frost
The critically acclaimed follow up to *October Snow*

After Awareness: Advocating For Battered Women
A handbook for community outreach

Printed in Great Britain
by Amazon